YES, YOU!

The fact is, hands have been sending important messages for a long time.

Public figures, Native Americans and characters from children's literature are among the most noted for using hands to communicate or to help make a point.

Perhaps the most popular signs are those used by people in sports. The umpire surely signaled gloom through Mudville that fateful day Mighty Casey struck out.

We all use hands to communicate in many ways. Waving, pointing, shaking hands and touching are only a few short cuts for speaking. Your hands probably have quite a bit to say:

Love at First Sign

SEVEN OUT OF EVERY 100 PEOPLE IN THIS COUNTRY ARE DEAF OR HEARING-IMPAIRED.

FOURTEEN MILLION PEOPLE! AMAZING.

I WONDER WHAT IT WOULD BE LIKE—NOT TO HEAR... I SURE WOULDN'T MISS MY SISTER'S CLARINET PRACTICE! BUT I WOULD MISS LISTENING TO THE HOCKEY GAMES IN THE CAR WITH DAD. AND WHAT IF I COULDN'T HEAR THE LUNCH BELL?

OR THE SOUND OF THE OCEAN, AND—

OUCH! HEY, WHAT'S GOING ON?

Are you a southpaw signer? You'll notice that all the signs in the book are made by "righties," so if you are a "lefty," simply switch them around to suit yourself.

PICTURE THIS

The language of signs is much more than a collection of random gestures. Each sign has a particular hand shape and a particular meaning. Some signs are easy to remember because they make a clear picture of the idea they represent. Banana is an a "peel"ing sign for this reason.

"PEEL" A BANANA

BANANA

CAMERA

TREE

SHAKE THE "LEAVES"

GROW

SPROUT YOUR HAND

22

TICKLE

KISS

SPIDER

HOUSE

25

Flying High

BODY TALK

What your face and body say while you're signing is just as important as what your hands say. No one needs an interpreter to know this sign means "angry."

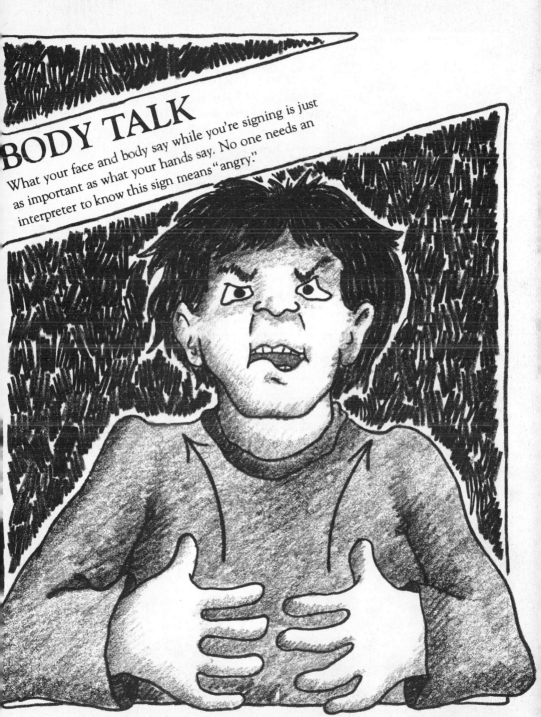

The exact meaning of a sign changes when your body language changes. Whether you have a "slight stomachache" or a "whale of a bellyache," you can use the same hand sign, but you must use different body and facial expressions:

t isn't always necessary to use a hand motion for "not" r "don't" because your face can say so for you. In fact, pposite facial expressions give opposite meanings to a ign.

Here's a puzzling problem: There's just one piece nissing, but there are two left and *both* of them fit! Which is correct?

By themselves, hand movements only tell part of the message. . .

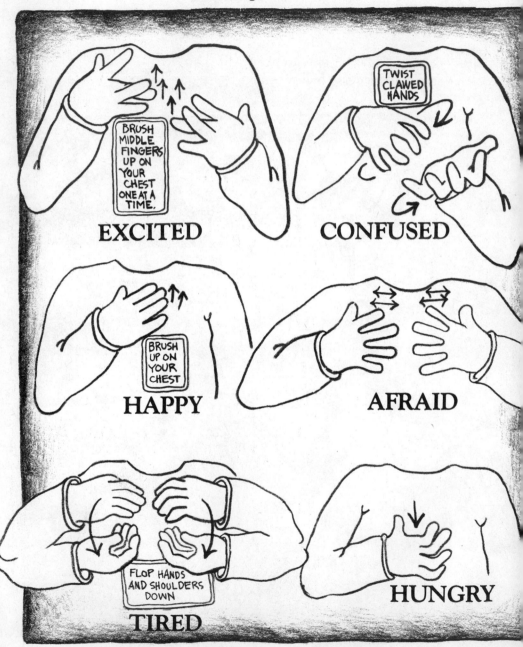

EXCITED

BRUSH MIDDLE FINGERS UP ON YOUR CHEST ONE AT A TIME.

CONFUSED

TWIST CLAWED HANDS

HAPPY

BRUSH UP ON YOUR CHEST

AFRAID

TIRED

FLOP HANDS AND SHOULDERS DOWN

HUNGRY

. . . but add a facial expression and you will understand
the whole idea.

Body language is important, but there's no need to get carried away.

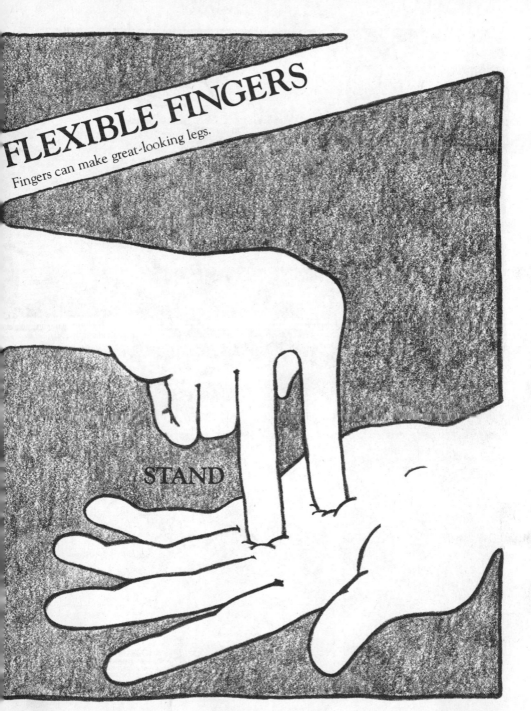

FLEXIBLE FINGERS

Fingers can make great-looking legs.

STAND

JUMP

LIE DOWN

KNEEL

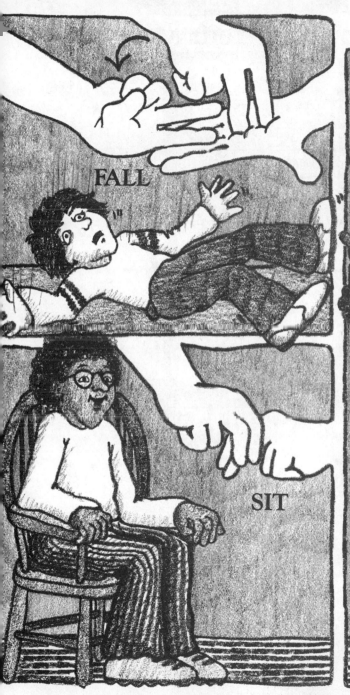

FALL

SIT

DANCE

There's a Spider in Your Milk

CELEBRITY SIGNERS

A few famous friends have dropped by to share their favorite signs.

MONSTER

LOVE

MOTHER

CUPID

TAP CHIN

43

SNAKE

MAGIC

STRONG

RAIN

NAME

NAME

MUSIC

45

Signs of a Perfect Day

SANDY'S ALARM CLOCK IS JUST ABOUT TO RING. A PERFECT DAY BEGINS IN HER DREAMS...

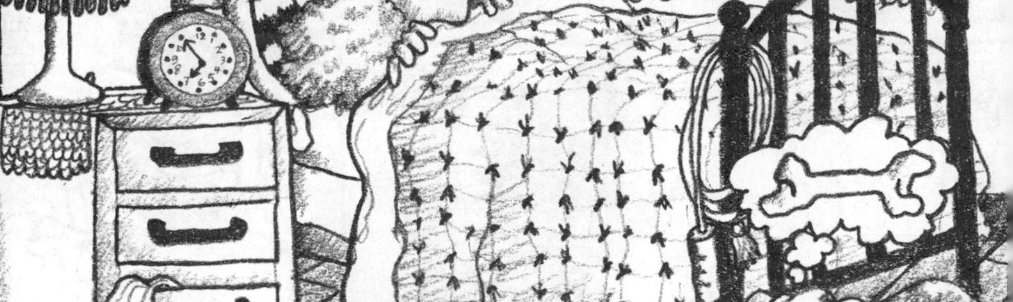

WAKE UP

PERFECT

DAY

DREAM

DOG

SHE EATS A YUMMY BREAKFAST AND READS THE "SUPER CEREAL COMICS." (SOMETIMES DAD PEEKS.)

SPEECH PRACTICE AFTER SCHOOL GOES SO WELL, SANDY LEAVES EARLY FOR TENNIS. SHE PLAYS BETTER THAN EVER!

SANDY AND HER BEST FRIEND, MARIE, ARE STARVING! THEY FINISH A MOUNTAIN OF SPAGHETTI IN NO TIME, AND A HUGE BOWL OF POPCORN "DISAPPEARS" DURING A CAPTIONED T.V. SPECIAL.

NO HOMEWORK! IT'S A MIRACLE! AHHH... TIME FOR A NICE HOT BUBBLE BATH. EVERYTHING IS PERFECT! BUT WAIT A MINUTE. SOMETHING'S WRONG. THE WATER WON'T SHUT OFF! WHAT'S HAPPENING?

FINGERSPELLING

Using 26 hand shapes, you can make all the letters in the alphabet and write them in the air.

WOW!

THE MANUAL ALPHABET

Try using this "airphabet" to fingerspell your name. You'll notice that many of the hand shapes actually look like letters.

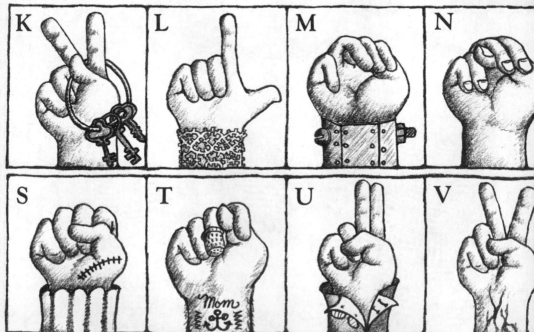

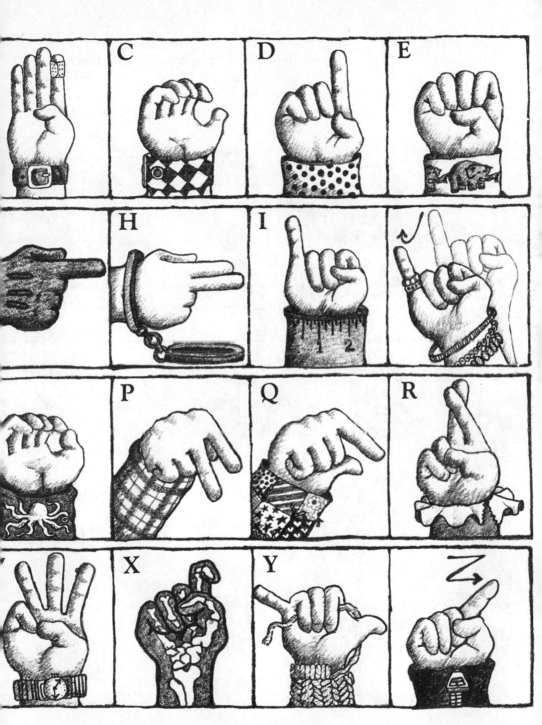

People have been fingerspelling for a long time, in fact since about the year 10! Bibles from that time show pages of alphabet hand shapes. Many monks of the middle ages, vowed to silence, used fingerspelling to communicate.

Fingerspelling is so easy, you can even spell "E-N-C-Y-C-L-O-P-E-D-I-A" with one hand tied behind your back.

Because signing is faster and more practical, fingerspelling today is used only for names, places and words that have no signs.

58

F IS FOR FRENCH FRIES

F is for French fries. You can make this and other
signs by moving the word's first letter in a particular way.

FRENCH FRIES

TAKE A FRENCH
FRY WITH AN F

JAM

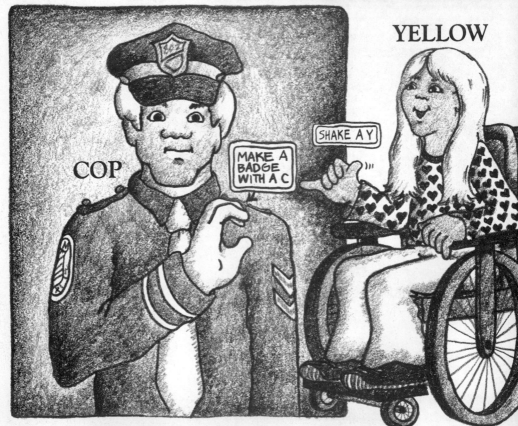

COP

YELLOW

OWL

WATER

TAP A W ON YOUR CHIN

VISIT

ROTATE 2 V's

LATER

PIVOT AN L FORWARD

RESTAURANT

BRUSH EACH SIDE OF YOUR MOUTH WITH AN R

DESSERT

TAP 2 D's

PERFECT

KING

MOVE A K ACROSS YOUR BODY

Signing Is a Cinch

65

Why I Learned Sign Language
By
Samuel E. Simmons

My name is Sam. This is the very first picture ever taken of my kid brother, Andy. He was so tiny when he was born that he had to stay at the hospital a few weeks before coming home. I didn't think he was so great. He wasn't much fun—All he did was eat, cry and sleep.

Here's Andy 2 years later trying to get the ball. I liked him better then. At least he could do a few things. He didn't talk and he never looked when I called him, but he was still O.K. at getting the ball. Mom and Dad tried to get him to say stuff, but he only made funny noises. What a kid!

Here's Andy having his first piggy back ride. That was right after the doctor said he was deaf. Mom and Dad were really upset about Andy, but we just kept right on playing.

Here's Andy gulping down his first ball park hot dog. Mom and Dad used to fight a lot then. Mom wanted Andy to learn sign language, but Dad said, "No way!" He wanted Andy to learn how to talk. He said sign language just wouldn't work.

Then one day Dad was watching me and Andy playing and he saw that Andy already used sign language of his own. It took a while, but Dad finally realized that signing was a good way for Andy to talk.

So that's why I learned sign language, in fact, my whole family did. Of course signing was a cinch for me right from the start! Andy goes to speech class now. He's learning how to control his voice to say some words. Last week he said, "Dad," and Dad signed back, "What?" That was a switch!

Andy really is an O.K. kid, but I still feel bad for the poor guy. It must be tough having such a great-looking older brother!

SIGN YOUR NAME

Anyone can have a sign name; just make one up! Most sign names use a person's initial to describe a special habit, personal trait or favorite hobby.

HI. MY NAME IS BOB. I'M KNOWN FOR WEARING MY HAT. IN FACT, I'M NEVER WITH-OUT IT. I TAP IT WITH A B TO SIGN MY NAME.

72

Meet Al, Gretchen, Carl and Mary Beth. Who's who?

I'M GRETCHEN, A PAINTER. I PAINT MY PALM BACK AND FORTH WITH A G TO SIGN MY NAME.

MARY BETH HERE. MY SIGN NAME IS MB.

MY NAME IS CARL. MY FAVORITE HOBBY IS MODEL ROCKETRY. MY SIGN NAME IS A C BLASTING OFF.

AL IS SUCH A SHORT NAME. I JUST SPELL IT OUT.

What's the Sign for Scary?

A CHOOSY WEEK

The sign for sneeze is not surprising, but did you know that people once believed a sneeze meant much more than just a tickle in your nose?

SNEEZE

Sneeze on Monday, sneeze for danger.

Sneeze on Tuesday, kiss a stranger.

Sneeze on Wednesday, sneeze for a letter.

Sneeze on Thursday, get something better.

Sneeze on Friday, sneeze for sorrow.

Sneeze on Saturday, see your sweetheart tomorrow.

Sneeze on Sunday, your safety seek,

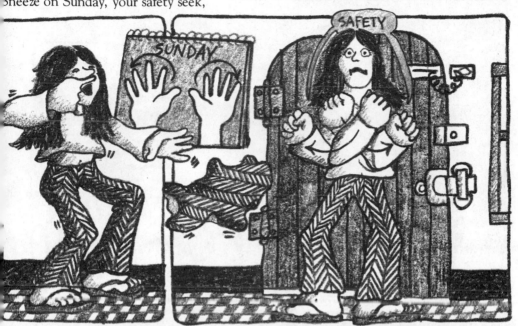

Or the devil will take you for the rest of the week.

83

HOW ARE YOU FEELING?

Whether you're feeling wonderful, curious, hungry or polite, you can be sure there's a sign for you.

WONDERFUL!

I'M FEELING POLITE.

YES

PLEASE

THANK YOU

I'M CURIOUS.

WHO? WHAT? WHERE?

I'M VERY SAD.

HEARTACHE

LONELY

CRY

WRING YOUR FISTS

I'M SO SILLY!

I'M HUNGRY.

I'M FEELING FREE!

KIDS SUMMER VACATION

Say It in Sign Language

SIGNING OFF

The best way to improve your signing is by practicing with people who use sign language all the time. When you do this, you will surely find that there is more than one way to sign certain ideas. You may also discover that some signs change over time or vary slightly from place to place.

There are more than 150 signs in A SHOW OF HANDS, but this is only a beginning. So, say it in sign language whenever you can and "watch" your vocabulary grow.

THE SIGNS